W9-BAW-093

TAKEN FROM THE RIVER

TAKEN FROM THE RIVER

POEMS

CAROL MOLDAW

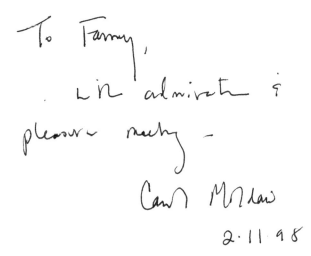

To Fanny,

with admiration &
pleasure meeting —

Carol Moldaw
2·11·98

MIDDLEBURY COLLEGE LIBRARY

Alef Books • *New York* • *1993*

Like easy conversation,
rambling, obliquely angled,
the winding street traverses
the steep residential hill.

Stone stairs ladder-stitch
the street's tiers; every few
landings open on terraces,
windows glinting through hedges,

sunlight feathering grass.
At the first switchback,
pine needles tufted with dog fur
pad up the wide cracked steps

leading to a cottage and two
ramshackle shingle houses.
From the lintel of an illegal
basement apartment, magenta

fuchsia, silent bells,
bob and sag over a pot's rim.
Higher, up wooden stairs
built over rubble, we climb

to the top deck. What was
our garden now grows wild
onions' white flowers,
and butter-yellow weeds —

winter's mohair throw
draping a bare mattress.
By late spring someone else
or no one will be bending

to pick cool herbs
like single guitar notes.
Something knots in my throat.
Indecipherable

decibels begin jackhammering
inside #D – our old address.
Black Sabbath? Iron Maiden?
I know our own records

by the first chord. Pounding,
we try the unlocked door,
and pick our way through
a year's domestic fallout:

dropped clothes, album sleeves,
mattresses blocking entrances,
plates, cups, hangers, books.
I trip trying not to look.

Waving on the balcony,
an old guest, now our host,
offers us the view.
At this time of year,

no yellow beach roses
tumble the latticed railing,
no draft of honeysuckle,
no bees flitting near their hive.

Cars nose around the hairpin turn.
Looking past Berkeley's hazy
flat grids, past Oakland,
you can see, as if you've flicked

a painted fan open, a striped
spinnaker crossing the wide bay,
three bridges, and San Francisco
shrugging off her damp negligee.

WHEN IT RAINS

we must be careful
to admit sadness.
For who is there to reproach us,
with our hearts in the balance?

Tonight it *is* raining.
I eat berries off your tongue.
Your hands join the stream
bathing my breasts.

Rain has no words
to console us, but I catch water
so your mouth will come close
to my cupped palms:

no one ever touched me
pained by such thirst.
Night flocks over us,
and, darker, the rain.

THE CALL

Back arched like an orchid branch,
open-mouthed, an orchid flower,
I was Sheba receiving Solomon.
You rubbed my thighs with myrrh.
I was twenty-one.

Soon I'll be thirty-two.
Your hands that know me well
hold me close like an earthen bowl
fresh from the potter's wheel.

When I made my wish
for love to last, that night,
on an indiscriminate star,
I was so sure of it —
trained and anointed by Ishtar.

A FIRST GARDEN

Last August, wild blackberry thorns
thrust through the strawberry patch.
The shaggy pine shook its needles
everywhere. Split and straddled,
they hung from an overladen plum,
and pumpkin vines lassoed it, trunk and branch.

Because memory is a weak thing,
I want that garden distinct as when
zinnias baked on our back deck
and three steps from the kitchen
door, walking through it,
I could see how tangled we'd let things get.

Twisted in thyme, parsley, oregano,
and dill, needles outnumbered herbs;
weeds outnumbered needles;
our garden strangled in the net
of minute flowers that stretched
across yards, threading down to a single root.

Some things didn't grow at all:
pepper trees a half foot tall,
cucumbers the size of olives,
my rosemary, your sweet basil,
catnip steamrollered by our cat.
Zucchini grew, prodding us under bristling leaves

while we watered and snapped off
pole beans abstractedly, nibbling
raw handfuls, stooping
low to ransack the fence. Duped
and captured by a first blush,
we'd been ready a month for a tomato to redden.

We had some unperplexing hours
there, by ourselves, bending over
strawberries as they sent out runner
after runner to cluster and flower.
How we lolled by that bed,
looking for berries so ripe and heavy they'd nod.

STANFORD HILLS

Tiptoe on a sturdy branch,
taller than the tallest girl,
she reaches into the sky

and pulls at a tangled thread.
Rows of clouds unpurl.
She can see miles ahead,

she can almost see Webb Ranch
across the tawny hills,
its silos, horse barns, fields,

and the two rickety shacks
where they buy vegetables
from Mexican women whose men

bending over harvest fields
fill giant burlap sacks.
She'd like to have a sack

to wear for Halloween.
She'd sew beads on the hem
and be an Indian maiden.

Bright feathers down her back!
Last year as Fairy Queen
in a tinsel diadem,

she waved her foil wand
and charmed the cul-de-sac.
Now she jumps, rolling beyond

cowflops, ants, a scraped shin;
flattened fields of rye;
her mother calling her in.

AT THE MAUNA KEA

Deaf to the sea stomping the beach
and palm fronds scissoring
the full moon, you were asleep,
so I stepped out to smoke.
The palms reminded me of Palm Springs.
The beach was cleaner than Acapulco's.

On vacation, family quarrels erupt
like a volcano. You divorced, me unmarried,
both touchy as virgins: touring Europe
in Mother's factory-bought Mercedes
that time we ate only spinach
in all the four-star chateaux.

Sister, as long as we're stranded here,
we'll be the surf's thinnest dresses.
When the tide empties under its curfew,
it's easy to turn a plastic shovel
into a bottle of pink champagne,
propped in a bucket of sand.

Once we saw the nest
outside our back window,
not three feet from the desk,
we kept the shade down.

The room, dark before,
took on a reverential hush.
Candles, incense, and
the Victorian mantel's crush
of I won't say what things,
were always offerings –
but the reds of carpet, chair,
and photo-enlarged saint
stepping off into thin air
seemed then a sacrament.

Not that anything was new.
But, strict in my routine,
oblivious as an ant,
like one of Pharaoh's slaves
never looking up –
I hadn't seen.

It was February and, we thought,
an odd place for a nest:
the fire escape landing.
Instinct, we had to trust,
led them to disregard
the stone pagoda's niche
(out of claw's reach)
and the dirt-packed planter's box
with its bonsai weatherguard,

constructing instead between
heat-and-cold-conducting
rail-thin wrought-iron bars.

Plump, contemplative
as Buddha, the wood dove
sat like a queen on her nest,
her charcoal-grey-brown breast
ballooning with each breath.
Sometimes her mate would perch
on a fire escape step
or the railing's balustrade.
We stopped using the porch
and kept the cat in,
but when I'd skirt the blind
to check on her, the slick
accordion-pleated plastic
draping me like a shroud,
she didn't seem to mind.
Her round unblinking eye
didn't seem to see.

Because we didn't know
how long eggs take to hatch
or when they'd built their nest,
I'd stop by the window
before making breakfast,
again before going out,
and right when I got back,
hoping all day to catch
sight of a gaping beak –
as if their choosing us
was presage, like spring's
first gaudy yellow crocus
that turns earth joyous.

Then one day she left
her eggs exposed. We saw
how uncushioned, threadbare,
and meager a nest it was —
like a bracelet of straw,
or a meadowgrass tiara,
something a daydreaming girl
plucking at weeds might weave
to crown her loosened hair.
At first I couldn't believe
the dove had left two eggs,
smaller than walnuts, pale
as spilt milk, to spoil
on our sill, but she had.

You cleared away the nest,
left it in Central Park.
I raised the blind,
opened the window a crack.
But even the sun's unfiltered
light hasn't lifted the gloom
that like dampness or dust
pervades the still dark room.

THE MOORISH BATHS

Housefronts decide
the curve of streets.
Inside wrought-iron gates,
a courtyard,
blue with flowers.

Enter the low door,
through the anteroom's
narrowing light.
Under jasmine-water
the floor dips
and disappears.

Listen: flutes,
drums, the gold chain
slung round a woman's
hips, and bells

murmuring on the
ankles of a eunuch
who brings wine
and pillows

while our shadows,
uncoiling toward
fields, blend
in the furthest furrows.

FOR A MARRIAGE

1.
This morning
the moon is white and round
and intimate as bone,

a bold, prosperous white,
porous, mid-sky. Hip to hip
we sit on the stoop.

The apprenticeship slips by.

2.
Love, you're well rehearsed,
but on that day, when we leave
my native town,

my father's house, what name
will you call to rouse me, to carol
and spirit me away

as I linger,
ungracious, furtive, a young girl
unwilling to stay or go?

JUDE:

My frenzies you call wildflowers.

A bridge and a stream
emboss the wide-brimmed China vase
where you arrange them.

PATRILINEAGE

The uncle's lopped-off head,
Cossacks in the sister's bed,
and the boy who hid, then fled,
took a name from the river
and crossed the sea, found
Ida, had you – who had me.

REB SHMERL AND THE WATER SPIRIT
A Hasidic Tale

Reb Shmerl, a peddler from Constantine,
thought he had found a way to sin
and keep his yearly slate as clean
as clouds, the suds God washes in.

He grabbed up sins at all his stops,
carted them home without a thought,
tossed them down the cellar steps,
slammed the door, and let them rot.

Shmerl raked up his sins each fall,
and stuffed them in a burlap sack
he rolled down to the lake, a ball
that sank like lead. The lake turned black.

"What does it matter?" he would say,
his hawker's hands thrown open wide,
as if to supplicate or pray.
"Whether I toss my sins aside,

or sink them in a capacious lake,
God magnanimously forgives."
He swallowed hard, two gulps, to take
his pieties like sedatives.

So sins, like gold coins, multiplied.
The once-clear lake, the dumping ground,
with black polluted spittle cried
and vowed someone would turn up drowned.

Reb Shmerl had only one regret:
his faithful wife could not conceive
what he somehow could not beget –
no son tugged at his woolen sleeve.

One day he walked from dawn to dusk
carting neither toys nor tools.
He sought the Baal Shem Tov to ask
if there was any truth to the tales

that he could intercede with God
and grant a pair so old a son.
(Shmerl's wife had given him the glad
thought to turn to this holy man.)

The Master pitied the peddler's wife:
"You'll have a boy, and that is all."
"What more have I asked my entire life?"
The Master stood. Shmerl felt ill.

"Remember this. For thirteen years
he'll grow, strong and swift as an otter.
On his birthday that year, as he is yours,
be sure he doesn't go near water,

or waves will carve your son's coffin
before he prays in synagogue.
Each year you've poisoned the lake with sin
and now it foams like a rabid dog.

That morning when you dress yourself
you'll put two socks on your left foot . . ."
("The Master's cracked," Shmerl smirked to himself,
blinking his eyes, tapping his feet.)

"By your bare foot, recall these words,
and remember to keep your son inside."
The Baal Shem Tov was good as his word:
their son was strong and steady-eyed,

everybody's favorite boy.
He liked to play all day at the lake,
riding on turtles, shouting "ahoy,"
or swimming, with fish flanking his wake.

The boy's Bar Mitzvah day was hot.
Early that morning his father woke
puzzled by a dream he forgot
entirely – like a half-heard joke.

Getting dressed, he began to fume
over a sock he couldn't find.
Searching, he hopped around the room,
but anger and effort struck him blind.

Finally, he shook his wife from sleep.
Her laughter like a town crier's bell
gathered neighbors in like sheep
to watch her husband before he fell.

"Where have you put my sock?" he cried.
"You've put them both on your left foot!"
She pointed – the townsmen, crowded inside,
all nodded at Shmerl's wobbling foot.

"I've WHAT?" he snapped, and the key turned
in its lock, the door swung open wide,
and the Master's words that he had spurned
rushed over him like a swelling tide

that rising knocked him down and seized
his heart, his son. His son. Was he
the only boy who had not squeezed
his way into the room to see

Shmerl fall? Shmerl's boy had overslept –
the scorching sun had woken him
with nothing on his mind except
the urge to take his morning swim.

As he ran past his father's door,
Shmerl saw him go and sprang to his feet,
scurried to catch him, begged, then swore,
but the boy raced on and crossed the street.

Shmerl called on God as his son slipped
on the slick grass and fell headlong,
his ankle throbbing, a tendon ripped.
"Get back inside, where you belong."

Shmerl gripped his arm to lead him home
and shouldered him like a sack of sins
until the boy stood up on his own,
Shmerl all the while muttering *Amens*.

The boy was locked in his room all day.
He begged but was forbidden water.
Worn-out, unable to get his way,
he slept and dreamt he swam in water

clear as glass and marble-cool.
He dreamt he grew enormous fins.
As guardian of the swimming hole,
he wasn't scared of the old man's sins.

By noon, heat made it hard to breathe.
Most villagers were down at the lake
when the water started to swirl and seethe –
boats were capsized in the quake,

but no one saw the spirit rise
until it thrust its hands in the air.
Black tears fell from its red-rimmed eyes.
Seaweed hung from its head like hair.

It searched from face to face before
any had time to reach the bank.
All heard its voice, like thunder, roar
"One is missing." And then it sank.

Watching his son's long sleep, Shmerl saw
the water spirit rise and claim
his boy as forfeit under the law
for the slew of sins that bore his name.

He knew them well and denied none,
repenting each, from first to last.
At midnight, when Shmerl woke his son,
the boy was hungry from his fast

and his ankle throbbed, but he was safe.
Shmerl's wife prepared the feast and set
an extra place by the large carafe –
the Baal Shem Tov would join them yet.

Sister, roll your hips.
The moon's full, a Chinese gong.
Roll your hips and aim a stone.
Aim for the bright bull's-eye,
the hammered brass plate
in the lake's dark sky.
Shimmy like that brass disk, sister,
shimmy till that pancake flips,
shimmy till the moon comes down.

LIFE

Poor Bob Rees died. Poor Bob.
Not the first of my parents' friends
to go. Hit them where they live.
That's God's way. That's life.

We die. We all die.
Someday we all may die
at the same time.
Anyway, we do,
moment by moment,
run down like batteries,
and some light's always going out.
Right now. Directly before
and directly after
Bob Rees. Poor Robert. Poor Bob.

A practitioner
of the most deliberate
arts, deflector
of spirits, interceptor

of wills, I toss
boys off course
for one night, one day,
an hour's hallucinatory

pleasures. Other women
use their charm to keep
their men; I use men
to keep my charms. Magic

thrives on man's embrace,
overarches earthly
inspiration to cascade
into one glorious vortex,

pool of all my best concoctions.

MENSES

Yesterday, a thread
of blood, a spool
unwinding; homespun
nubbed yarn, red
saturated strands I
wound round my finger;
tacky, silky, wool;
moon-cloth, harbinger
of no one, unwoven.

Juice of the crushed
pomegranate seed,
disintegrated nest,
floating egg freed,
dam burst and flushed
clean in the spring
tide's flux; slowly
draining watery breast;
everything aching.

Sacred curse men fear,
too deep to discuss,
ochre we daub and smear,
the lunar calendar's
primary ink: thirteen
ruby moons a year
flowing from fertile hips
flower on soft lips,
poppy, rose, hibiscus.

THE CROSSROADS
for J.B.

One moonless night I gather yarrow stalks
and bring an obsidian disk to the straight-backed chair,
poised and topaz-eyed, like a red fox,

for auguries, angry skirrings in the air,
the gravel path up-scuffed, a streetlight blown.
But what clarifies in a candle's sudden flare,

a long thin nose and pointy chin, is my own
three-quarter silhouette, dispersed
head-on, the way water's shattered by a stone.

Once I would have swallowed back my thirst,
sulking like that scrawny black cat I gave
milk to last spring, who made me woo her first.

But now it's my Mother's long black cloak I'd have,
Her glistening skullcap of stars, Her brindled pack,
as I stalk the earth, rounding it like a wave.

Midnight. No moon loops the zodiac.
Drugged, she sleeps dreamless in a dark cave,
one kitchen match to light her way back.

Her voice bristled in my ear
even today as I pinned my hair.
Already it's been over a year
since the penetrating stare

of her dark eyes commanded me
to bloom, or wilt, because I saw
in her an age-old authority
whose blink, blessing or curse, is law.

A year is nothing. Time stands still
for those asleep in the dreamers' cave,
those mesmerized by ritual,
and those to whom the Oracle gave

no definite answer, but a kiss.
Smoke rises from the fissure's mouth.
The twining snakes rub and hiss.
What good can come from North or South?

Wind that unravels knotted smoke
rips the intricate skein apart.
I can't fix what the winds broke,
or piece together my heart.

DELUGE

Tears like arrows falling
around me in the midst of battle.
And after the battle, how I've wept,
how love has made me weep.

TO —

Birds all about me —
none knows which way to flock.
If only, having read my letter,
she would call . . .
Should I leave another message?
Say, this is how it is with me,
my heart, the letter fluttering in your hands?

FROM ASSISI
for J.O.

1.
Candles at Vespers
and blazing torches;
booms; lulls; whispers;
alternating bells;
far and near churches.

2.
Like a rose window,
the round moon rose
above the basilica.
What face did she show
to him, in Africa?

3.
Medieval, but urban –
archways and alleys
plastered with comets;
the straw magi's
fluttering turbans.

4.
Awakened, lovesick,
to tribal drumming
in my Umbrian attic.
Clear synchronicity –
and then more static.

5.
A bevelled mirror,
a vanity for a desk;
books halving the bed;
fog, dawn and dusk;
figs, oranges, bread.

6.
An unfinished Flight
in a hillside chapel,
hidden from sunlight
behind a bare altar,
near Eve and her apple.

7.
Following sheeptracks,
taking turns at the helm
of Melina's carriage,
talking of home,
art, poetry, marriage.

8.
Doves flocking for seed
flung from a satchel
every day at noon
beside Minerva's Temple
in the Piazza Commune.

9.
Studying frescoes
of Francis preaching
to the attentive birds;
casting the I Ching,
weighing its words.

10.
Squeaking bicycles,
housemaids' quarrels,
wheelbarrows, a rooster,
sheep and church bells,
heard from my cloister.

IT WAS THEN

You were pleased to be alive;
not yet used to love,
to me, eager at your glance.
It was winter. I can see
you striding through the snow
at midnight. Something inside me
shifted. Made room.

TO M.

How will I name the signal image
we traveled hot to find?
Am not star-gazer, herb-seeker,
dirt-tiller; am not one who
recognizes which bird sings
what keen note on the branch
of which tree – but ignorance
serves me: I cannot stray
or straying will not wrongly
give my heart's address.
Name star, name flower,
field, bird, branch. Name twig,
scrap of twig, seasons, and
name years. By you I know
the world, and what once was
nameless, love, I call by name.

When your father died
his hair was blown
all to one side
and his mouth kept
the shape of his breath.
It too looked windswept,
oval, not round.
The lack of sound
when his breath stopped
was itself a prayer
absorbed by the air.
A gentle death.
He was light as a seed.
While he labored to breathe
you stroked his arm
and searched his eyes.
He held your gaze
as though, now freed
from human ties,
he could look at you
from closer at hand
and not risk harm.
All that was left
in his eyes was love.
They were clear blue
cornflowers faded
the color of stars.
Before they were closed
his chill gaunt face
once so bereft
was swept with grace.

Packets of seeds, lobelia, cosmos, and phlox,
meant for a bedroom's redwood window box,

seven years, two states, three apartments back,
still rubber-banded, a neat rattling stack

stashed under paper clips in my desk drawer.
I remember going to the garden store,

its greenhouse windows fogged with thick moist air,
the hanging ferns, the delicate maidenhair,

big water-stained clay pots, rustling bamboo,
birdbaths, broad-fanned palms, a cherub statue,

the yellow hoses coiled to strike like snakes,
the shovels, pitchforks, hoes, and gangly rakes.

Late afternoon southwestern light would splash
that bedroom window and bounce against the sash,

dappling the leaves and air before it fell.
Some days a few drops leaking in would swell –

light absorbing light in shallow pools
that slowly sank into the floor. Time fools

with things, but how light changes stays the same
year to year: the August sun that came

to fill our window box with cardamom light
must be lengthening on the ledge, though here it's night

and the full moon gapes behind her billowing curtain,
her face half-hidden, her attitude uncertain.

– But I bet she reads me like an open book.
She must have seen my schoolgirl's lead-eyed look

staring back at her a zillion times
while I restructured love's component rhymes.

Tonight's no different. Fingering those seeds
like loose freshwater pearls, or worry beads,

I see pink cosmos whirling on its stem,
and, as if we'd really planted them,

the phlox and midnight-blue lobelia overspill
onto the bed. I'm trying to keep still,

and not to laugh till you're through sketching me –
a charcoal flagrant with expectancy.

THE WATERCOLOR
for S.E.

The thinnest most adventurous
strokes trail the hills and cross
the horizon, cross the handdrawn
blurry border and (they are trees)

seem to sway, abandoning
the cultivated landscape
to lean over the uncropped
outskirts of the page.

Two trees pierce the horizon.
The field is lighter, greener,
than the orange-yellow hills
a stream divides with the same

wintry blue as the white sky.
One of the three flowers
is you say a heart and who's
to disagree – it's yours and visibly

suggestive, even to the blackness
at its core. A heart enough like
any other, a flower in a field, a spot
of blackness deepening the red.

Not extraordinary that strokes
are trees, but these are
yours, of the same ink and hand
as the stream's bank, the hill's

ridge, the border trees trespass,
and the flower like a heart
I keep coming back to because
at the black center it bursts.

TRANSMARINE

An open hull nudging reeds and sand,
she kept to herself the pleasure he provoked,
the undercurrent dimpling as he stroked,
and drifted, slackly moored under his hand.
Turning to him, she let him loose the knot,
drop the rope, and push his foot against
the pier to lift her free. Her muscles tensed;
he took her like a sail the wind had caught
and guided her until she guided him,
and when they were no place that either knew,
where sky and sea and shadow echoed blue,
they plunged – and were knocked back at the world's rim.

IN MEMORIAM
FRANKLIN WALKER III
1954–1988

1.
Some days you slept through my visit,
your eyes not quite closed, but your breath
even. Leafing through *Vanity Fair*,
or *Spy*, whichever you'd requested,
I'd squirm in the squeaky leatherette chair
and finally sleep if I wasn't rested,
my legs stretched out and my feet tucked
between your mattress and the bed guard.
Sometimes you'd sort mail while we talked,
sitting up, your knees sharply bent,
your checkbook sliding down your thighs,
another well-meant get well card
splayed open and pitched like a tent
on the foothills of your sloping sheets.
One time, when Bunny brought you sweets –
imported, creamy, wrapped in foil
and eagerly devoured – I shrank
to see the empty box on show,
as if it were dark chocolates, Frank,
that made your T-cell count drop low.
Somehow I thought it more loyal
to frown on what you shouldn't eat
and cook brown rice with miso soup
(a Jewish daughter's chicken broth),
as if the food you wouldn't eat
could make you strong. To think of it.
To think how I used to criticize
most what I loved, the extravagant cloth

and substance of your obdurate self,
the cashmeres, leathers, silks, all stuff
both of us prized and coveted,
which you admitted and I did not.
Lanky in your hospital gown,
your high black cheekbones hollowing,
the IV's curling tendril dug
like a thorn into your wrist, your nails
turned black and ridged from AZT,
you wondered how the odds broke down –
would they invent a miracle drug?
Would you survive past thirty-three?

2.
Your patients think you have a cold;
you keep appointments on the phone.
Your parents think you're out of town.
Only closest friends are told.

Potted plants, fresh cut flowers,
friends who call from overseas,
and friends who visit at all hours
lift your spirits by degrees.

Both men and women nurses flirt
because you're sweet as columbine.
Outside your room's a "Danger" sign:
contagions present; red alert.

Needles go down a special slot.
Linens into a covered bin.
Across the way, doves in a dovecote
burble and coo, as you grow thin.

Blue masks protect you from our breath.
The staff's equipped with rubber gloves.
It's part of life, outwitting death.
The columbine's named after doves.

A dovecote is a columbary.
A columbarium's a shrine.
You grow more skeletal and weary
until your skin begins to shine.

3.
One afternoon I took a cab
from Mount Sinai to a psychic on Fourth.
We inched through midtown rain and traffic,
zigzagging between lanes, edging
forward sideways like a crab.
Blocking jaywalkers near St. Mark's,
the driver, clearly psychopathic,
warned me away from weirdos, punks,
and other vermin I might meet.
Then he sped up and lurched to hit
every pothole in the street.
Below his rearview mirror, dice
entangled rosary and cross.
I thanked him for the free advice
and rummaged in my purse for change
though thinking only of the loss
to me if you should up and die.
He must have found my drawn look strange.

The front room was an unkempt shop –
boxes of dusty crystal points
stacked on milk crates against one wall;

the glass display case countertop
crammed with bowls of tumbled quartz,
amethyst eggs, and tigereye.
I looked at chips of opal, jade,
a garnet in its granite matrix,
emerald, turquoise, aquamarine.
Polished amber, light as a leaf,
warmed my open hand. A ball
of deep blue gold-flecked lapis spun
a double helix up my spine –
or was it just the shivers when
I heard distinct derisive snorts
and someone tapped me from behind?
It was a balding snub-nosed man.
He led me into an inner room.

Jeweler's scales stood on the desk.
Bottles of tincture lined the shelves.
He said to sit, to close my eyes,
align my higher and lower selves.
Looking past me, he read my aura,
then accessed the Akashic Records,
a kind of karmic accounting book,
flipping through pages in his mind
with fervor, like a student of Torah.
I blurted out your name to ask
the fates how I could help you live.
He cut me off with a look:
"His eyes won't close until he's died.
You're neither mother nor lover, although
in a past life he was your son.
It's not your place to be his guide."
It startled me he mentioned your eyes,
as if that was too much to know.

Too much for me to know. Too much
while you still live to think of death
as your new friend, the rest of us
forgotten. "Fake it till you make it,"
you would say. So I try
to picture you, your red bow tie,
your quick uptake no one can touch;
the way my forehead reached your waist;
the time we rode an all-night bus,
and how, that once, we kissed. I play
the years backwards till we meet.
The cafeteria. Noon. You've just
woken. Your roommate's girlfriend waves
and introduces us. I taste
it all again and let the years
build up with visits back and forth
till we both live in the city and
I'm standing on the street in tears.

4.
A yellow shaft of light
hovers above your bed.
You watch it with delight.

The dust motes swirl and dance.
Your rapt dreamy look
catches me off balance.

Standing near your bed,
I'm talking on the phone,
not hearing what is said.

I watch you lift your hand
and turn it in the light
as if you hold a strand

of pearls – and now I lose
the phone call's slender thread.
The sun's full on my face.

The caller doesn't pause.
Slowly you move your hand
and with your fingers trace

the sunlight in my hair.
Your palm brushes my cheek.
I say I'll call right back.

Our fingers interlace
and make a latticed sieve
to cup the buoyant air,

scooping light like sand.
Days later you are dead.
The roses for your grave

are yellow like the sun.
Like light, like air, you live.
We drop them one by one.

Your friend heard my mute song's
thin stream on the hikers' path
and knelt. Whorled and knotted,
charred, arching, furled
like a wave, sinuous as smoke,
I fit her grasp – a hook.
Now you have me, *your genie*,
and my song sticks in your throat.

A five-inch wisp of wood,
propped on your desk three years
while you pieced together scraps
of repeatedly x'd-out words
describing how the hole
bored clean through my left eye
and the right's curved lid-line
make me seem half asleep

and half haunted, a skull.
I don't want to wait anymore.
My goat-mouth, a crosshatched,
nicked slit, is always open,
my windpipe's air hole exposed
above its tongue-flap,
a foreshortened arm flung wide
while, chanteuse, I hold my note.

Writing these words I've put
in your mind to put in my mouth,
certain no one will see
what you see, daunted, you drop
your pen in despair and pull
from the drawer a strip of black
Egyptian cotton cloth
to bind and muzzle me.

I only pray it's days,
hours, not weeks and months,
till you have heart enough
to take me up again –
though not one splintered strand
of my ram's-horn headdress,
my two high-piled topknots,
will meanwhile whiten or uncoil.

AED-1227   12/19/01

PS
3563
O392
T3
1993

ABOUT THE AUTHOR

Carol Moldaw was born in Oakland, California, and grew up
in the San Francisco Bay Area. She was educated at Harvard/
Radcliffe and Boston University. She lives in Pojoaque, New
Mexico, with her husband, Martin Edmunds. *Taken from the River*
is her first book.

This book was designed by Emily Singer and printed on
Mohawk Superfine by Becotte & Gershwin, Horsham,
Pennsylvania. The cover was printed by Anne Noonan at
SoHo Letterpress, New York.

Alef Books are published in association with the Educational
Alliance, Inc., New York.